Field Trip!

Nature Museum

Angela Leeper

Heinemann Library
Chicago, Illinois

Designed by Kim Kovalick, Heinemann Library; Page layout by Que-Net Media
Printed and bound in China by South China Printing Company Limited.
Photo research by Jill Birschbach

08 07 06 05 04
10 9 8 7 6 5 4 3 2 1

Library of Congress Cataloging-in-Publication Data
Leeper, Angela.
  Nature museum / Angela Leeper.
      p. cm. – (Field trip!)
Includes index.
Summary: Introduces a nature museum, exploring who works there and what they do, different types of exhibits, and other things to do in a museum.
  ISBN 1-4034-5164-8 (HC), 1-4034-5170-2 (Pbk.)
  1. Natural history museums–Juvenile literature. [1. Natural historymuseums. 2. Museums.] I. Title.
  QH70.A1L44 2004
  508'.074–dc22

2003014526

Acknowledgments
The author and publishers are grateful to the following for permission to reproduce copyright material:
Cover and interior photographs by Robert Lifson/Heinemann Library

Every effort has been made to contact copyright holders of any material reproduced in this book. Any omissions will be rectified in subsequent printings if notice is given to the publisher.

Special thanks to our advisory panel for their help in the preparation of this book:

Alice Bethke
Library Consultant
Palo Alto, California

Malena Bisanti-Wall
Media Specialist
American Heritage Academy
Canton, Georgia

Ellen Dolmetsch, MLS
Tower Hill School
Wilmington, Delaware

Special thanks to the North Carolina Museum of Natural Sciences and the Peggy Notebaert Nature Museum in Chicago for their assistance in the preparation of this book.

Contents

Some words are shown in bold, **like this.**
You can find them in the picture glossary on page 23.

Where Can You Learn About Animals?

You can learn about animals from books.

You can also go to a nature museum.

Museums collect and show things.

A nature museum collects and shows animals.

What Is a Docent?

docent

A docent works at the museum.

He shows you around the museum.

A docent tells you about
the animals.

He also answers your questions.

What Is an Exhibit?

curator

Exhibits show what the museum collects.

A curator helps take care of the exhibits.

Signs tell you about the exhibits.

Some have buttons you can push.

What Is a Diorama?

Dioramas show where animals live.

This diorama shows where a bald eagle lives.

This diorama shows where a
deer lives.

What Kinds of Live Animals Can You See?

You may see butterflies and moths.

These moths are eating fruit.

cocoon

You may see butterflies come out of their **cocoons**.

What Other Kinds of Animals Can You See?

You may see pond animals.

You may use a **microscope** to see them.

You may see **reptiles**, too.

This snake is a reptile.

What Kinds of Animal Homes Can You See?

You can look inside this log.

Ants, mice, and other animals live inside.

You can look at this beaver's home.

A beaver's home is called a lodge.

What Can You Touch at the Museum?

You may touch some of the animals.

This turtle has a hard shell.

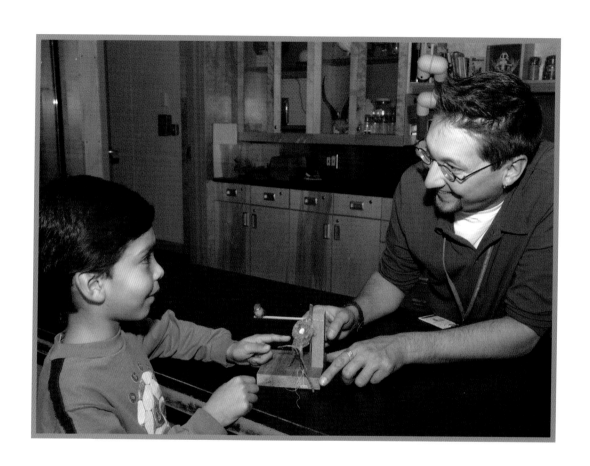

You may touch animal homes, such as a shell or a nest.

This boy is touching a tiny bird's nest.

What Else Can You Do at the Museum?

You may watch a movie.

It tells you about the **exhibits**.

You may dress up like animals.

These children are dressed
like beavers.

Museum Map

pond animals

bald eagle diorama

microscope

bison diorama

beaver lodge

deer diorama

butterfly exhibit

Picture Glossary

cocoon
page 13
covering that keeps an insect safe while it changes shape

diorama
pages 10, 11
kind of exhibit that shows a place where an animal lives

exhibit
pages 8, 9, 20
something you see at a museum that teaches you about something

microscope
page 14
tool that makes small things easier to see

reptile
page 15
kind of animal with scales on the outside of its body

Note to Parents and Teachers

Reading for information is an important part of a child's literacy development. Learning begins with a question about something. Help children think of themselves as investigators and researchers by encouraging their questions about the world around them. Each chapter in this book begins with a question. Read the question together. Look at the pictures. Talk about what you think the answer might be. Then read the text to find out if your predictions were correct. Think of other questions you could ask about the topic, and discuss where you might find the answers. Assist children in using the picture glossary and the index to practice new vocabulary and research skills.

Index